Visit and Learn
National Memorial for Peace and Justice

by Susan Glick

FOCUS
READERS®

BEACON

www.focusreaders.com

Focus Readers is distributed by North Star Editions:
sales@northstareditions.com | 888-417-0195

Produced for Focus Readers by Red Line Editorial.

Photographs ©: Brynn Anderson/AP Images, cover, 1, 4, 25, 29; Shutterstock Images, 7, 11, 12, 17, 19, 22, 26; Library of Congress, 8; Julie Bennett/AP Images, 14; Andi Rice/Bloomberg/Getty Images, 20–21

Library of Congress Cataloging-in-Publication Data
Names: Glick, Susan, author.
Title: National Memorial for Peace and Justice / by Susan Glick.
Description: Lake Elmo, MN : Focus Readers, [2024] | Series: Visit and
  learn | Includes index. | Audience: Grades 2-3
Identifiers: LCCN 2022055608 (print) | LCCN 2022055609 (ebook) | ISBN
  9781637396193 (hardcover) | ISBN 9781637396766 (paperback) | ISBN
  9781637397862 (pdf) | ISBN 9781637397336 (ebook)
Subjects: LCSH: National Memorial for Peace and Justice (Montgomery, Ala.)
  | African Americans--Monuments. | Slaves--Monuments.
Classification: LCC E185.53.M66 N384 2024 (print) | LCC E185.53.M66
  (ebook) | DDC 976.1/47--dc23/eng/20230105
LC record available at https://lccn.loc.gov/2022055608
LC ebook record available at https://lccn.loc.gov/2022055609

Printed in the United States of America
Mankato, MN
082023

About the Author

Susan Glick lives in Maryland with her husband. She loves writing for children. She reads mystery stories for fun. She also likes to kayak in rivers and marshes. The Chesapeake Bay is nearby. She walks along the shore and finds sharks' teeth and fossils.

Table of Contents

Chapter 1

Here to Honor

People stroll quietly to the top of a hill. They stop to look at a **sculpture**. It shows enslaved Black people in chains. It is part of the National **Memorial** for Peace and Justice.

Approximately four million Black Americans lived in slavery in 1860.

The memorial is in Montgomery, Alabama. At first glance, it looks like a city park. But it is much more. The memorial honors Black people who were **lynched**. They were killed by mobs of white people.

The main square is filled with monuments. Some hang from the ceiling. Others stand on the

Did You Know?

The monuments list thousands of names.

> The monuments are made of steel. Rust makes them turn brown as they age.

grass. Each monument tells where a lynching happened. It includes the names of the people who were killed.

Chapter 2

Building the Memorial

The idea for the memorial started in 2010. It began with a group called the Equal Justice Initiative (EJI). Lynching wasn't something many people talked about. So, EJI wanted to know more.

 In 1882, a mob lynched Frank McManus in Minneapolis, Minnesota.

EJI's members read stories in old newspapers. They traveled to places where lynchings happened. They talked to families. They talked to people who knew history.

EJI learned that thousands of Black people had been lynched. They counted more than 4,000 **victims**. These crimes happened between 1877 and 1950.

EJI decided to build a memorial. The group bought land in Montgomery. An **architect** helped

 Montgomery is the capital of Alabama. In the 1950s, the city became the center of the civil rights movement.

with the **design**. The memorial was built outdoors. It had flowers and trees. It also included sculptures.

 The memorial includes more than 800 monuments.

The memorial told the stories of the people who were killed.

A main square stands at the top of a hill. In part of the square, the floor slopes down. Visitors look up.

The monuments hang above their heads. Each one is as long as a person. This shape makes visitors think about how Black people were hanged from trees.

The memorial reminds people of a terrible part of US history. But it tells the truth.

Did You Know?

The United States has many memorials to people who died. But Montgomery has the first national memorial for people who were lynched.

Chapter 3

Eager for the Truth

The memorial opened in 2018. People came from all over the United States to see it. Some visitors were surprised. They did not realize so many Black Americans had been lynched.

 Congressman John Lewis was a civil rights leader. He visited the memorial in 2019.

15

Some visitors did not know lynching had happened in their own counties.

Visitors read the stories. They learned that Black people were taken from their homes. They were killed without **trials**. Some visitors looked for the names of their own relatives.

The memorial got people talking. Reporters wrote newspaper stories about the memorial. Videos of the memorial were shown on TV. People

 Each monument includes names of people who were lynched.

began asking questions about their own communities. They wanted to know if any lynchings had happened there.

17

EJI helps communities learn more. Some communities want their own memorial. Or a community might want a marker to put by the road. It can tell about lynchings that happened there. EJI helps write the markers. Markers are a way to tell the truth. Markers honor the people who suffered and died.

Did You Know?

Most lynchings happened in the daytime. The mobs were not punished.

NON SIBI, SED ALIIS

GEORGIA HISTORICAL SOCIETY

Mary Turner and the Lynching Rampage of 1918

Near this site on May 19, 1918, twenty-one year old Mary Turner, eight months pregnant, was burned, mutilated, and shot to death by a local mob after publicly denouncing her husband's lynching the previous day. In the days immediately following the murder of a white planter by a black employee on May 16, 1918, at least eleven local African Americans including the Turners died at the hands of a lynch mob in one of the deadliest waves of vigilantism in Georgia's history. No charges were ever brought against known or suspected participants in these crimes. From 1880-1930, as many as 550 people were killed in Georgia in these illegal acts of mob violence.

Erected by the Georgia Historical Society, Lowndes/Valdosta Southern Christian Leadership Conference, Valdosta State University - Woman and Gender Studies Program, and The Mary Turner Project

2010.3   92-2

 A roadside marker in Georgia describes lynchings that took place in the area.

EJI's goal is to make sure lynching is no longer a secret. The memorials speak out against **injustice**.

The Legacy Museum

The **Legacy** Museum is a companion to the memorial. Inside, **holograms** speak for the enslaved. Actors recorded the voices. Their words come from writings that enslaved people left behind.

Visitors can stand in front of a slave pen. A hologram woman tells a story. She is crying for her children. They have been taken and sold.

The museum also celebrates many heroes. They fought against injustice. Their stories can inspire visitors.

EJI founder Bryan Stevenson stands outside the Legacy Museum.

Chapter 4

Visiting the Memorial

The memorial is a quiet place. For some visitors, it is sacred. They talk softly. People walk slowly around the square. Helpers walk around the memorial. They can answer questions.

Approximately 600,000 people visited the memorial in its first year.

Visitors read the names on the monuments. They read the names of counties and states. They read the stories on the walls.

There is a water wall for unknown victims. Visitors listen to the sound of water. They think about the people whose names are lost.

The sculptures outside are reminders of the fight for justice. A sculpture honors Rosa Parks. She and others fought for justice on city buses. Another sculpture shows

 A statue called _Raise Up_ shows victims of racist violence.

Black Americans with their hands in the air. Their bodies are stuck in cement. The sculpture shows that violence has not ended.

FOR THE HANGED AND BEATEN.
FOR THE SHOT, DROWNED, AND BURNED.
FOR THE TORTURED, TORMENTED, AND TERRORIZED.
FOR THOSE ABANDONED BY THE RULE OF LAW.

WE WILL REMEMBER.

WITH HOPE BECAUSE HOPELESSNESS IS THE ENEMY OF JUSTICE
WITH COURAGE BECAUSE PEACE REQUIRES BRAVERY.
WITH PERSISTENCE BECAUSE JUSTICE IS A CONSTANT STRUGGLE
WITH FAITH BECAUSE WE SHALL OVERCOME.

 The memorial helps make sure the victims of lynching will not be forgotten.

Visiting the memorial can be a powerful experience. A reflection space gives people a place to sit and think. They might need to talk about what they've seen. Some people feel deep sadness. Others feel angry. Some are confused. And some people regret not knowing about lynching.

However, many visitors also feel hopeful. They hope things can change. They hope lynchings will never happen again.

Did You Know?

The reflection space honors writer Ida B. Wells. In 1909, she called lynching a national crime.

FOCUS ON

National Memorial for Peace and Justice

Write your answers on a separate piece of paper.

1. Write a letter to a friend describing what you learned about the National Memorial for Peace and Justice.

2. Why do you think lynching wasn't talked about for many years?

3. When did the memorial open?
    A. 1877
    B. 1950
    C. 2018

4. Why are some lynching victims unknown?
    A. EJI didn't know how to spell some names.
    B. The names weren't written down.
    C. They were lynched in the dark.

5. What does **inspire** mean in this book?

*The museum also celebrates many heroes. They fought against injustice. Their stories can **inspire** visitors.*

    A. make people feel afraid

    B. make people feel hope

    C. make people confused

6. What does **sacred** mean in this book?

*The memorial is a quiet place. For some visitors, it is **sacred**. They talk softly.*

    A. having a spiritual or religious meaning

    B. having an unusual shape or color

    C. having a frightening look or sound

Answer key on page 32.

Glossary

architect
Someone who designs structures and makes construction plans.

design
A drawing or plan for a project.

holograms
Three-dimensional pictures that are produced by lasers.

injustice
When something is unfair or violates someone's rights.

legacy
Something that is passed down from what came before.

lynched
When a person is killed by a mob without a court deciding if the person was guilty.

memorial
A structure built to remind people of a specific person or event.

sculpture
A piece of art that has height, width, and depth.

trials
Processes in courtrooms to decide whether people are guilty of crimes.

victims
People who have been harmed.

To Learn More

BOOKS

Duster, Michelle, and Laura Freeman. *Ida B. Wells, Voice of Truth*. New York: Henry Holt, 2022.

Gonzalez, Maribel Valdez. *Choose Justice*. North Mankato, MN: Capstone Press, 2023.

Loh-Hagan, Virginia. *Racial Justice*. Ann Arbor, MI: Cherry Lake Publishing, 2021.

Smith, Elliott. *Slavery and Reconstruction: The Struggle for Black Civil Rights*. Minneapolis: Lerner Publications, 2022.

NOTE TO EDUCATORS

Visit **www.focusreaders.com** to find lesson plans, activities, links, and other resources related to this title.

Index

A
architect, 10

E
Equal Justice Initiative, 9–10, 18–19

H
holograms, 20

L
Legacy Museum, 20
lynching, 6–7, 9–10, 13, 15–19, 27

M
markers, 18
mobs, 6, 18
Montgomery, Alabama, 6, 10, 13
monuments, 6–7, 13, 24

N
newspapers, 10, 16

P
Parks, Rosa, 24

R
reflection space, 26–27
reporters, 16

S
sculptures, 5, 11, 24–25

V
victims, 10, 24
visitors, 12–13, 15–16, 20, 23–24, 26–27

W
Wells, Ida B., 27